Yvonne Williams

# *Broken*
# Men/Women
# SHOULD
# NOT DATE!

SUPPORTED BY
REST RENEW
RESTORE
MINISTRY

Trilogy Christian Publishers

A Wholly Owned Subsidiary of Trinity Broadcasting Network

2442 Michelle Drive

Tustin, CA 92780

For information, address Trilogy Christian Publishing Rights Department, 2442 Michelle Drive, Tustin, Ca 92780.

Trilogy Christian Publishing/ TBN and colophon are trademarks of Trinity Broadcasting Network.

For information about special discounts for bulk purchases, please contact Trilogy Christian Publishing.

Manufactured in the United States of America

10 9 8 7 6 5 4 3 2 1

Library of Congress Cataloging-in-Publication Data is available.

ISBN 000-0-0000-0000-0

ISBN 000-0-0000-0000-0 (ebook)

# Acknowledgments

To Yvonne Williams

Thank you for all your spiritual blessings of wisdom and your undying love for the Gospel words of Christ. It's your persistent prayers for the family and for all who love the Lord Jesus Christ. I thank you for being a blessing in my life and our Ministry in Beth EL Worship Church. I want to encourage you to continue to increase your faith in Christ and never change who you are to those of us who love you.

Love you always,
Your Husband
Pastor R.C Smith Sr.

Don't let what you see make you forget what I said. -God.

In all you do, do it with God. Always lead by faith and not by sight. Reading this book, I've learned that knowing someone's past can truly humble someone's present and future.

(Loving heart mojo)
Love you, Mother Sherice

This is a story every young woman needs to hear before she settles for worldly expectations. My mother's story will remind you that our God did not create you broken, so don't spend a single day living as though you are.

Thank you for sharing your story, Mom. – Tiara

As a seasoned woman, this book is a blessing to me and will be to others. Ms. Williams, your obedience to God and transparency shows us there is no situation God cannot bring us through.

This book reminds us to continue to trust the Lord and keep the faith. Continue to be a blessing to others. Thank you, and I love you.

-Sandra Durham

# Table of Contents

# Wow: Groundswell

I know the title might make some people angry, but if you can give me your attention right now to stop and listen, then I have accomplished half of my purpose in writing this book. I have stopped and started this book many times over almost twenty years. Take just a moment and answer a question. Are you at the top of the wave of joy as if you're on water, surfing through life? Or are you having a groundswell moment where you're at the part of the wave that has not broken you yet? Or lastly, are you broken and need some support quickly? Well, I'm so glad you have the book in your hand.

Now that you have the book in your hand let's talk.

# Filling My Alabaster Bottle

I know you just knew this relationship was going to work. You put your all into it. The keyword *you* put your *all* into it. A successful relationship takes two people and God. I don't understand. He was tall, had a job, and said the L-word after our second date. Stop crying. All these things sound like they loved you, although these attributes sound great. They're superficial if both parties are not in it to win it for a long-term commitment. Oh yes, you have heard this before, and you still feel like you can put in more time, and they will change into the person you want them to be. Others might change themselves for a while to appease you, but their character will not keep them in the relationship for the long haul. Please don't blame yourself totally for the list you have made for the individual you want to stay in your life. The person we want in our life is a collective individual created from how we were brought up. Another part of that person is the opposite of who hurt you in your youth. We seek affirmation in those who say the right thing without observing the potential pain before letting them into our hearts. "Above all else, **guard your heart**, for everything you do flows from it" (Proverbs 4:23, NIV).

You're not telling me anything new. I felt the tug at my heart when thugs or things didn't line up. I would ask how your day and the reply was would come out as another question, and we would get sidetracked. Still, I allowed the flow to carry me to a safety zone area for the moment, and that special person would smile, which restored the belief in my mind that they loved me. Some have said, I will settle for *bozo* unless and until Boaz arrives. Zero people can take up space and hold no value. The number zero is powerful only when an actual number is at the beginning of the number. You cannot take 00,000 money to the store, . You will buy nothing. However, with a 5 in front of 00,000, then with $500,000, you can truly go on a shopping spree. Let's stop right now and listen to the Holy Spirit. You can go on the shopping spree with the money and the following month be screaming because now you have the bill, and it is all meaningless because these purchases only have value in the natural. They do not fulfill the spiritual thirst that no earthly possession can quench.

You might say, "I'm not a religious person." We all were created in the image of God. We consist of water, blood, and flesh. A doctor can name the other items. We can choose not to accept our total package, but it will show up when your character takes it somewhere, and you can't stay there for long because you will feel empty again. How do you know these things are true? What're your credentials? What college did you go to? Okay, slow down! I'm going to be transparent with you about my story called life. I'm just going to ask you along the way to be transparent and honest about what you feel as we travel through my past. Can you do that for me? Now, we might pass each other on the street or even live in the same state. However, if we ever met, you probably wouldn't forget me. Those close to me say I never meet a stranger. It's not a game I play. It's truly genuine! It's innate for me to flow in a positive mindset! It can be sickening to some. Some have said to me, "Do you wake up every morning smiling." Yes, I smile from the inside! My flesh will attempt to follow the flow in times of rebellion, but eventually the flesh gets on board.

I have allowed my spirit man to be in control of most of life because if you think about it, the creator gave us that which allows us to wake up! Yes, I have a strong overflowing relationship with God. He knew me before my parents even came together. "For you created my inmost being you knit me together in my mother's womb (Psalm 139:13, NIV).

I must take you back to the beginning because I want you to trust me. I'm welcoming you into my deepest memories, and I pray that you will trust me enough to share some of your hurts so we can heal together. If you are a youth and life is still so wonderful, please regift the book somebody else. I don't want another generation to wander in the wilderness of life for years when they could instead enjoy and remember a trip that could have been learned in a shorter period.

# Watching

He left me!

My father has his issues. But he was the only father that I had known in that capacity. This experience would dictate how I would handle all my male relationships in the future. unless I trusted God totally. We know a dad can create a strong foundation that will help his children soar like eagles in every area of their lives. A confident child can be a successful president of their own company or a nation. See, success is a faith attribute that will create expectation throughout life's journey. As a child, no doubts exist, only dreams and peace. But dreams and hopes can only be replaced when adults don't reinforce the child's desires.

I remember when I was in first grade, my father would pick me up sometimes from school. Since I'm reflecting, my father must have been picking me up a lot recently because on this day, I felt disappointed that my mother came instead. A mother's love has a special place in a daughter's heart, but it's a deeper feeling when you experience a man's affection, no matter how small the package it might be. I had learned at an early age to appreciate the small morsels of affection. But remember, this sets the tone for all of your relationships!

My father was stern. He disciplined us when we came short in our obedience, but I remember him buying me a bicycle. He gave me a short period to learn in his presence, and when it became apparent that I still wanted the training wheels on, he came back to me and disciplined me, stating that I must go outside and not come back in until I could ride my bike without the training wheels. As a child, I thought this was harsh, but later in life, maybe just recently, I realized this lesson that created within me a strong will for a strong future: To make it no matter the odds against me. Dad was dealing with some demons, and he didn't see any solution for a positive outcome. He had the spirit of endurance even if he didn't use it. Seeds can be planted in any soil. Yes, I learned how to ride my bike that day, and I can't tell you how long I was outside that night. As a side note: dads, when you give projects to your children, care enough to check on them even if no one ever checked on you. My father didn't have an earthly father to check on him. He had just started his relationship with God, and he didn't have the faith to trust Him fully. Time ran out for my father, so he didn't become the best father or husband for his family. See, an abusive person might one day be healed, but he can hurt so many people so much in the meantime.

# Observation with No Action

I experienced death at a young age, and I had to grieve in silence. I remember leaving our apartment, taking an elevator downstairs and when I walked out of the building, I saw what appeared to be a lady not breathing by the corner of the wall. I could feel death. She was laying there, still, with a needle stuck in her arm. This life was not the life I wanted for myself.

One day not too long after, my life changed forever. I can remember my mother walking me home from school. I ran into the house and looked for my father and found him in my brother's bed. He appeared to be asleep. No, he was cold, and he never responded to my voice. I was removed from the room. I went into the kitchen and sat down. I can remember nibbling on the leftover bacon on a saucer as I watched the paramedics removing my father from the house for the last time. On that day, a trend began as people leaving my world and leaving me broken in my spirit.

My grandmother came a few days later. Several family members who I had never seen before came to our home from all over the country. Everyone was sad. I don't remember the service or the burial. They probably kissed me and hugged me more that period of my life than any other time in my youth. The hugs and communication became limited because everyone went back to their own world. Why does it take someone passing to bring out compassion? I was told many years later that the main issue that hit my father's life was an untruth about him. Those issues, which had something to do with the military, were corrected and he was reinstated, and honors given back to him after he passed! Wow! This unnerved me in my adult life.

This nugget of wisdom taught me to love unconditionally. See, people's praise is okay, but it will change if you later don't measure up, and they will take back the compliment and the love.

At a young age, I started a true relationship with God. He became my soul-saving grace. God's love through Jesus Christ became my saving grace. Yes, I said it twice. I'm feeling His loving grace right now. Thank you, Jesus!

Please understand when my father left my life, I was told not to discuss the manner in which he left us. I was instructed to say that he was in the service, and many people would just fill in the blanks. Only a few would linger for more information, and I would say he was ill.

Being in a prominent family has some disadvantages, and you're taught not to be transparent. "What happens in the home, stays in the home" was our brand. We handled our misfortunes with a smile, and you continued to fill your alabaster bottle with your tears.

We no longer had a television, and we soon didn't hear soul music or any other secular music. We went to church every night after Christian school. Now, let me tell you I enjoyed the only life I had known. The church was multicultural. I was raised in a world that was colorblind. We respected one another based on how they made us feel in their presence.

I learned to play the piano and sign language. My brother learned to play the saxophone. We were exposed to the arts in our youth. I love going to an opera! I think my first concert was a Cinderella opera. Afterwards I was given a baby grand piano. I had recitals. I played Bach and other classic pieces. I didn't learn about the other sex due to our religion. I knew that our God was not the mean spirit that some portrayed Him to be. I felt His love and discipline through faith. My greatest strength as a child was learning how to pray. Through my prayers, my soul would be cleansed through an overwhelming number of tears. At times others translated these moments as a sign of weakness. Please let me reassure you I didn't become a weakling when I cried or still cry but my strength came in that way. It was so heavenly. I must say, life was full of learning Bible stories of how man and woman made it through life. The Bible became my best book.

Now, let me tell you I loved to read. The library was my haven. I could travel to numerous countries and learn about their culture without buying a ticket. It was so economical to travel back then. With all the restrictions on my life, I survived because of the wonderful relationship with God that had evolved since I was seven years old. Jesus never left me. I answered the phone with the words "Praise the Lord," and a lot of times the other party would just hang up after they started to laugh. Another hurt was placed in the alabaster box. I was taken out of PE because I refused to be picked on for wearing a shirt over my shorts. I was raised so different than most of the children. My life youth also has some good memories. I love the drama classes at school, and I love participating in the church plays. I played the role of Mary in our Easter and Christmas productions. Parents, stop working so much and visit your children's' schools. Don't just go for PTA meetings. Surprise your children by going to lunch with them. You can be in their story in a beautiful way. You can smell the roses of life with them. Let them experience a limo ride other than to a funeral! Plan for special moments, or life will plan for you.

As a young girl, God would talk to me and strengthen me through many situations. I could feel His presence in nature as the wind would brush across my face, and I would pass the warmth of love to others despite any woes that had happened in my youth.

Although I felt the wind on my face, I had not learned how to clean out the hurt inside my heart. I had learned how to suppress any negative pain by locking it in my alabaster box.

I can tell you we had wonderful Christmases. We had so many gifts that we couldn't see the furniture in the room. We would get toys and our winter clothes for the new year. We were exposed to literary arts, from operas to classical music. My mother even took us to see a movie. Now you may say, so what was the big deal? Well, we soon joined a church that didn't allow us to have a television in the house and attending plays and operas was against the rules.

Yes, I'm smiling as I share my story. Although these memories were great, they didn't empty my fears and hurt lingering in my alabaster box.

# Attracting the Right Person

What piece of knowledge would I give to our youth of this day and time? If you're only a taker and don't give of your time and respect to others, then you will not be satisfied in your soul as a young adult. Where you plant seeds is where they take root, and weeds will stem up in all areas in your growth. Bad seeds will make tough vines of bitterness and choke out kindness and love. Start with what you like in your character. For example, if you like to be clean and have an attractive appearance, volunteer your time in a senior citizen's home and help groom them. Or if you love numbers and money, then give time to educating the Boys and Girls' clubs or YMCA. You will appreciate life in a mature way. Parents, start by having your children help you and other adults. Have them clean up after themselves and help with chores without a handout of allowance. I can remember my husband giving advice about the children, but I must paraphrase so I won't come across as rude. "The children didn't ask to be here, and it's our job to give to them whatever the cost!" However,

I have a Biblical comeback response that I never said out loud in my home or to my own, the children didn't ask to come, but while they are here, I'm going to teach them about the grace of God, and that it should not be taken for granted. I allowed my actions to be the true way of raising the children God lent me. Remember they're only lent to us!

We were all created before we ever conceived them, and the only one who had to die for them was Jesus. Your children aren't going to kill you with selfishness and conditional love. The children are to be raised with guidance and love. Raise the children with the Word of God as their foundation, and they'll never depart from Him. I'm not talking about man's practices that were so stern that a young child doesn't know how beautiful they are, and when the first guy tells them, "You're pretty," they give him their sweet thing.

Mothers, I don't want the young girls to be raised like me. I was not able to show my knees. Also, when I started to develop as a young woman, my clothes had to be worn loose and not revealing. Why did I have to hide the gift of the body? I remember a young man saying that I had a great figure, but that particular dress was removed from my closet, and I couldn't go outside if my parents were not at home as a teenager, lest I be admired from afar. Not just any boy could talk to me.

Now we couldn't date because you could tarnish

the name of the family. So, we girls suffered in silence or sneaked away to a park for a soft kiss. Some of us survived by going to college with dorms, while others like me went to a school without and stayed home. While at home, I still was attached to a young man, but we never went on any official dates. Not that we didn't see each other at family and church functions. Now, I can confess that we did steal away at the parks before choir practice. Did the adults attempt to save their name cause some of us had a lot of ignorance in relationships? You're now a young adult learning your way but hoping and praying that your foundation will hold you through the strong winds of turmoil.

A young guy needs to be honest with their intentions, and young ladies should be thinking about their future. Be an acquaintance, not a friend, and go out in groups. Stay in sports and clubs at school. Have a man earn a friendship. "Why!" you might think, "You're so old fashioned!" I'm glad you have your opinion, but I have lived longer than you.

If you have not experienced what I went through, stop the relationship because I don't want you to waste your time with a zero-worth relationship. Remember, zero has no value but takes up space. I know you have heard people say, don't bring sand to the beach. When one is still seeking a partner, then they will not take the zero with them.

A man should not start dating until they understand what they want out of life. Just remember, when a man is dating, they are walking with and sharing with someone else's daughter. Would you like your daughter to be treated that way? What way are you talking about? Sure, I will explain. When you stand her up for a date or don't say what you are really feeling, then you're hurting her. Remember, every person wants to be liked and loved.

I remember a woman who knew a very intelligent man who was totally focused on his career and made it known by his actions that dating was not an option. The woman went on with her life. When the gentleman had become successful in his career, he noticed a missing piece of his heart. He reached out to her. She had been working on herself and was whole with so much confidence that she let him know that she still had feelings but needed to be dated for a season. They're married now and serving others in every way.

We need the truth! Angels will sing in your soul! I have watched, and at times, I myself have been asked to hold off and wait for a call or a man to make a decision, but I've always have continued to make my own plans in my life. Kingdom business has always been a top priority!

The following season of my life consisted of learning the Bible, which I still love. God had grace and mercy. Learning Bible stories of how man and woman made it through life was a strong influence on my survival. The library was my haven. With all the restrictions on my life, I survived because of the wonderful relationship with God that had evolved since I was seven years old. Jesus never left me.

By adding good attributes to your character, you start chipping the ice off your alabaster box, and healing can begin. Or you can be like I was and keep the lock on the box, but while building a good and loving person on the outside.

Remember others are observing you. Men are visual, and they dwell on appearance. My appearance was beautiful and a giver from the heart. No, I'm being honest. I love deep because I was truly applying what I was being taught at church.

# I Deserved It

Okay, here comes the guilt trip that we all put on ourselves when we experience abuse. I deserved it! Let me say this only one time: you never deserve to be hit physically or mentally.

The reason I can tell you that you don't deserve it, is because I told myself that I deserve the road I had traveled, and I needed to suffer in silence. Because I did this, I want to fight harder to make sure other young ladies and young men don't have this story. I want you to have a wonderful life that doesn't include an Exodus of leaving Pharaoh and God having to open a miracle like the Red Sea to get you to healthy and prosperous life.

> *Jeremiah 29:11 (NIV) states, "'For I know the plans I have for you,' declares the Lord, 'plans to prosper you and not to harm you, plans to give you hope and a future.'"*
>
> *So, "Wait for the Lord; be strong and take heart and wait for the Lord." Psalm 27:14 (NIV).*

Let me continue my story of what not to do! Now, I had been an okay high school student because I feared my mother in that she would not spare the rod if I didn't.

## HE SLAPPED ME

I married at a young age. I was about to be a junior in college. No, I wasn't pregnant, but I was asked. He vowed that I could finish college and be married at the same time. Oh, no, it didn't happen the way I planned because we were both broken in spirit. He thought he was losing me, so he broke up with me, and then he wanted me back, and proposed and I accepted. Fast forward: our life started to involve other people without my knowledge until I would aggravate him when I was being nice!

He was fighting an internal battle, and I was releasing my baggage of frustrations. The strange thing is that it came out in the craziest ways. He would make requests without following through with instructions, and one day he slapped me. He blamed me for his action, but I didn't hear his response because that slap plunged me back into my childhood, where I saw abuse. The pandora box or my alabaster box had opened my memory, and the music it played was a dramatic horror story. I didn't speak while he was driving home, but when we arrived at our home in his car, I quickly ran into the house, packed a bag, and drove off in my own car. My mother taught us to always have your own car and a checking account only in your name. I took hold of the car wisdom but trusted him enough to share all of our bank accounts which later was a disadvantage. I didn't have a smooth financial transition into single parenthood. I know I left out a lot. Okay, you want me to go back. When he slapped me, it was early in our marriage, no children yet, and I had only completed one more semester of college. When I left the house that day, I didn't go to friends or family, but to a hotel. I called him and informed him never to put his hands on me again and hung up.

People say there are two sides to every story, and that is true, so when to my surprise, when we went to our pastor for counseling, we only discussed giving my husband peace of mind of where I was that night. So, I was instructed to take him back to the hotel, and the manager confirmed that I was there by myself. The slap was not even acknowledged. You say I should have gotten out then, but women didn't have rights back then, and our church didn't believe in divorce. What? Yes, it's hard to believe. We stayed married, and we had children. What I didn't know was that we still had others attached to our marriage. I had a few signs through a list of incidents that happened after my last child was born. I had to go to the doctor and obtain medicine for an infection that I knew I had not caught out of the marriage. One night my children and I became very sick, and when I called his job, I was informed that he was always off on that day. I never addressed this until one day, when I came home to use the restroom and found him sleeping with the other uninvited person in our bed.

I had to wake them up, and his reply was not to hurt her, and then he said something. Please wait for it. He pulled way back into our secrets we had only shared and released a whopper! He stated, "I am going to kill myself." Let this marinate in your mind. Why is this so devious? I will tell you in a moment because I'm taking a moment to relive the tragedy with a healed heart and mind. I don't hate anymore. I can truly say you can get through it! I wish that is where the story ended. I'm holding myself as I try to hold back tears, but they're coming anyway.

No, I didn't kill them. I went downstairs and called his family and stated that they were needed because of their child's intentions. I hung up and left home. Now you're saying I left him. No, I was counseled that we were going to get through this if we kept it all quiet because of our status in society!

Yes, I screamed within for almost a year, and started leaking from life. At times when I was angry, I was given medicine in the form of words, "Why are you bring up the past? You stayed with him." Those words resonated so deep in my subconscious that one day my brain and heart just broke down. I just remembered pulling over to the side of the road. I didn't recall where or how long I was there. All I could do was cry out to God and ask for His help! God, if you allow me to get home. I will no longer take the physical and mental abuse and make a new life even if we had to go under new names.

Let me tell you, even at my lowest state, I knew God could reach down and restore my memory to reality. I was in the deep. I was going to the spirit for strength.

Yes, my life changed, and it grew worse! I was held at gunpoint a couple of times. Sugar was placed in my car tank, and I was followed everywhere! This was just his way to remind me that I wanted the divorce, and I would not have a peaceful life. If I can't have you, then nobody will!

I chose to stay in the relationship, but soon I had to leave for my children and my sanity.

My alabaster broke, and I had to deal with my own hurt of my father leaving us at a young age. I had to cry until I was cleansed with the oil of joy that started to flow out of my alabaster bottle of life that God had for me. My inside began to reflect the joy that had always shined from the outside. See, although people thought I was a spoiled child and that I had never been through hard times, at the same time, I was suffering from some terrible memories.

Take off your mask and allow yourself to be healed. See, God was there all the time, but He gave us the choice of asking Him for help.

# Beyond Broken

Now, my life didn't change for the good right away. So, I must continue to reach a few more of you who think that God doesn't care even with the situation that you're in right now. Hug yourself. Stand in front of a mirror and say with me, I'm beautiful, and I do matter.

I want to ask you a question, Once you get beyond broken and you are healed, will you help someone else get to a safe place? Will point them to Jesus Christ? Or will you be silent?

The more you understand that your journey is not about you, but to ask for Gods' love, the more you can use the hurt for a ministry to restore others.

Broken is a state of mind. You were once a whole person with faults, and you are feeling shattered into pieces that can be brought back to wholeness through the Holy Spirit and your fight through faith!

I *know* you might feel like the Shunammite's woman

that didn't need anything. (2 Kings 4:8–28). Allow me to paraphrase. She and her husband were well off, and she set up a room for the prophet who would travel through their town, so he had a place to sleep. Well, she had been so good to him that he had his servant inquire of what the lady needed in her life. The servant came back with a report of her great wealth but that she didn't have any children. So, Elisha prophesied that at that time next time next year, she would have a son. Remember, He had watched Elijah, and now he had a double portion. What is your need from God?

I know you have been blessed and that one desire you have kept hidden in your alabaster box that you wouldn't dare ask for because you don't want to be disappointed. Just in case God wouldn't give it to you. You say, "I'm living in the season of abundance," or you might be an individual who thinks that you have done all great things on your own. I must say to you, keep on living. There is a time and season for everything. Read the entire book of Ecclesiastics.

God said to Satan, have you considered my servant _____? Fill in your name.

I must share that I have been living a good life. I have been blessed with great jobs and no need for anything. After all the sadness I experienced in my marriage, I forgave him, and we are nice to each other.

God asked me to start a ministry after I made a pilgrimage to Israel. I was obedient, and He blessed the gathering. This led up to the pandemic.

How do you learn to *rest* in this beautiful world after all the hurt and bruises of the past?

_____

_____

_____

_____

_____

_____

_____

_____

_____

_____

_____

_____

_____

_____

_____

# Wisdom and Knowledge

I'm glad you took some time to answer the previous question. I want you to pray over your response, then go back in five days, reread the question, and answer it again. Next, pray and fast about your answer, and then answer the question again. See, the world is thirsty for living water, and we know Jesus, and we are just getting by? I want you to have your first love event with God again.

Wisdom and knowledge should be a marriage that holds your breath and makes you want to have an everlasting relationship with God Almighty. Because if the relationship continues to grow and fruits of your labor are produced, others will want what you have, and you will not have to speak to the story. Just live the story out until God calls you home.

# Bozo versus Boaz

Now, I can tell you that this is the turning point of the story and how I know from my personal experiences that broke men and women shouldn't date. I have interviewed hundreds of people from people in college, young couples, married couples, and seasoned couples, and the similarity is that they are thankful for their ex-friends and bozos that are no longer in their lives.

College students informed me that they're still not totally supporting the title of my book because if they don't date broke men, they will not have anyone to date. It makes you think! Are we setting ourselves up for the stone age of women being the bosses with a stick? Let's think about it. Please note, in today's world, young men are seldom working part-time jobs in high school. Do they save their money? When they go off to college, are they working as they complete college? And do they pay tithes of the money they do make? Most of the answers I received were *no.*

I have a wonderful ending to this part of my life. This is also why the book wasn't published three years ago because I didn't like the ending that I had before. Three years ago, I was still working crazy hours and alone. I would date, but the relationships were shallow. The men were either looking for someone to take care of them or friends with benefits. Both choices didn't last long, and I was determined not to settle for a bozo and wait for my Boaz. For those of you that don't know who Boaz is, please let me tell you a wonderful story from the Bible. The story is in the book of Ruth, in the Old Testament, and I will paraphrase. However, please make time to read the entire book.

Ruth had been married to Naomi's son. Naomi had been in the overflow of great wealth in Bethlehem, but then a famine came to the land, and her husband and two sons' left and lived in Moab. Ironically, the abundance of food was in the sinful country, but God has a plan even when we have weak faith. Fast forward, Naomi's story was sad, like my story for a long time. Her husband and both sons died while in Moab. Out of desperation, Naomi decided to move back to Bethlehem and begged her daughters-in-law to stay in their homeland. She had two main reasons. First, Moab women wouldn't be welcomed in Bethlehem because of their rituals of giving small children to their gods. Secondly, Naomi had become bitter with old age, and she wouldn't have any more children. She had forgotten the promises of God. We all have come short of the glory of God. Don't worry. The story gets better. Naomi finally grants Ruth's request to go with her. and she gleans in the field of plenty. Because she listens to her mother-in-law's guidance, she, later on, marries the man who owns the field she once gleaned in. Look at our God. Here is an example of how we should be listening to the young generation, for they too have their knowledge, and then they will receive our wisdom. Can I hear an *amen*?

# Sowing and Reaping

I pray that you are in one of your favorite places while reading this part of the book. Yes, stop and find a comfortable spot. This spot might be your prayer room or your sanctuary. Grab a blanket. When I had allowed my cup to get half empty with joy, I had to stop and regroup and start the process of refilling my cup.

God gave me a demonstration that I use when I'm teaching or speaking.

I ask my audience to have seven cups and a pitcher of water. Next, we fill the cups with water to reflect how the last seven days of their life have been flowing with the joy of the Lord. I would have them look at the cups and reflect upon the water in the cups. If they need to change the water level in any of the cups, they are free to do so. If any of the cups are overflowing, I ask them to drink from the cup to refresh themselves because it's their cup. What is so interesting is the response I receive from these groups. I have had some who are content with the half cup of joy days and felt the joy of other cups overflowing. I have been told that the overflow is from where your joy comes.

Can you stop and obtain three cups and fill them with water and reflect on the last three days of your life and how much joy you had in each of your days?

The last time I did the exercise, God spoke to me and said to remind the group of the Parable of the Ten Virgins (Matthew 25) and remind the ladies to keep their lamps full of oil. We are in a time when the world will test us, and we must stay full of joy and full of the Holy Ghost so that no matter what happens, we will not curse God. The Bible says that there will be a great falling away in the last day, so, let us sow day and night, then we can reap a great harvest. Also, the world needs to see our fruit. The fruits of the spirit are in Galatians. We are going to prosper in the last days. The meek shall inherit the earth.

Notes:

_____

_____

_____

_____

_____

_____

_____

_____

_____

_____

_____

_____

_____

_____

_____

_____

_____

_____

_____

_____

_____

# How Much Did It Cost Me?

Let me tell you, while the tears start to flow down my cheeks. It was worth it to say goodbye to my ex-friends and bozos. My marriage problems flowed into not trusting guys for a long time and to be silent with God for a while because He promised never to leave me.

Please hear me: After years of being alone and friends walking away from me before God brought the right friends to be in my life. I prayed for marriages to stay together and fasted when the marriages didn't work. I was alone when I celebrated ten and twenty years at one company and then eleven years with the second company. I asked God why and even asked Him if I could at least meet my companion, and He told me that "he is not ready to love you the way you are supposed to be loved."

I often said that a man was not going to want my life because of how much God had blessed me. When the pandemic hit in 2019, I was told I had cancer, and if it had not been found when it was, that I would have died quickly. I did get COVID-19 and was sick to death for over four weeks. Now, I must tell you that I had moved to a city where I didn't know anyone, and God had truly blessed me with a beautiful home. So, if I didn't tell you, except for being off work a lot, you would not know I had cancer. My doctor wouldn't give God the glory but was so amazed that I found cancer, and it was removed. Now, I'm told the area next to where I had the surgery was has cancer cells, but I'm still claiming that I am cancer-free in Jesus' name.

When I was given COVID-19, I fought to live every day. I have asthma, and breathing was a chore every day, and with two infusions that had me throwing up, diarrhea, and no sense of taste, I lost over thirteen pounds in a week.

# Rest Your Body and Use Your Money Wisely

God allowed me to live to tell the story so that you can get just a remnant of hope from my story.

I lived on edge for years. I couldn't save money like I was raised to do. I was a single parent, and every dime had to be accounted for to survive, and at times some looking into my window of life would say said to me, "at least you had credit cards," but years later, I had to pay for the credit cards through a lot of sweat and tears!

One thing I did start doing during this time was taking trips by myself and one with the children. These trips sometimes consisted of just seeing a movie, but other times, I would save for over a year to enjoy a real trip to somewhere I could drive, Florida. See, the power is in your hand, and only with faith in God can you conquer any mountain!

I started small. Saving money in a 401k and paying

my tithes was my fountain of overflowing blessings. I'm being real. It didn't happen overnight. I cried in my room many times, but God used my children to speak life back into me. Raise up a child in God, and he will not depart from it. It's in their roots. Just keep praying and praise God that it is already done! Take a piece of paper or your phone right now.

On gross income, set aside the following out of your earnings:

10% tithes. Trust God

5% Offerings/Charities

5% Pay yourself

5% Short term events

5% Long term events

Pay your minimum on all of your bills except one. If you are discouraged, then start with a small business and build your faith.

Are you ready to start the process? You may say, no, I'm fine because I have already saved $50k, or yes, I'm starting this process on my next paycheck. Yes Lord, this is confirmation of what I need to do, and although I can't do the entire process, I'm going to start praying and pay my tithes, and God, you're going to open blessings for me and the next four generations.

Surround yourself with true prayer warriors, ones you can be real with, to whom you can say "I failed," and they don't hold the story over your head but just pray. Don't put people on pedestals that you don't want to be judged on because you might be pushed off that ledge of life.

Prayer and fasting are the weapons of our warfare. The devil knows if he keeps us busy, we will not rest our minds. So, you can make better decisions. Rest your heart so you can heal from brokenness and then date somebody who has learned how to rest and not argue in their spirit when the battle comes because it will come. When the time comes, the Word says, you have everything within your reach to win in the spirit, which will overflow into the natural.

# Renew Your Mind

When you look at the word *renew*, you must first face that some things have become old, and you want it new again. I had survived physical and spiritual abuse, but I was still existing.

Let me tell you that a relationship with God will keep you through anything! Okay, how can I share a sad event in my life? I was saved at a young age, sang in the choir, acted in church plays, later in life, taught Sunday school. Okay, no angel, but I married and had children. I tell married women when God placed in my spirit to share: here it goes. I blamed myself for the failures in my marriage, like why did I live so deeply, why I wasn't handling his physical needs, etc. One day I worked in the field close to my house and decided to take a lunch break. I entered my home, and it was very quiet, but my husbands' car was outside. I investigated my bedroom and noticed my husband sleeping with the oldest child. His arm was around her. My heart is racing still as I write. I didn't disturb them and chose to use the hallway bathroom instead of the master bathroom. However, as I was in the bathroom, it hit me that the cheek of the female was larger than that of a child. I remember washing my hands and walking back into my bedroom, standing there. I finally woke up my husband! The minutes following influenced our marriage, leading to our divorce years later. I can tell you that I needed to be renewed in trusting another human being.

Now, after the incident, we stayed underneath one roof. It was dangerous because I wanted a divorce but was told if he couldn't have me, then nobody would. Some family members tried to help me, and some obtained warrants to protect themselves from him harming them. I was isolated at church and with family. But God! I said yes, and my God became my best friend.

I know some of you have been where I have been. You, too, have lost children, self-confidence, and income. Whatever your loss, you too can be renewed in body, soul, and spirit.

I have been angry with God. "Are you going to leave me too!" He said, "No, my child. You have a choice to trust me to remove your mountains and start with a small amount of faith in Me."

Now, I'm being transparent with you. Can you take a moment to say, "I'm going to allow God to renew me in my situation." If you're not ready, then I'm asking you to set this book down. I love you, and you need your time to mourn! God has you!

# Restore Your Dreams

When people meet me, they always determine that I'm younger than I really am. I used to be bothered by it, especially when I was dating because I was usually attracted to older men, and they would say at one time or another, "You're just too young for me!" I was so mature for my age because of what I had been through. On the other hand, they didn't believe me when they found out how old I was. God had restored me! I was carrying my past pain on my appearance. Look at our God. Now, my hurt would come out in me telling my story! Let me tell you: We had a motto that whatever happened in our home stayed in our home. Those walls of fear kept you in bondage. I care too much for you, do not live a godly fulfilled life! This process of restoring your life is determined by your will to surrender your hurt to God. I was told that when you can talk about the hurt and don't burst into tears, then you're truly healing! I know I am healing every day.

# 2017-2021

I'm dating not as a broken person. I take on the spirit of transparency! If I meet someone and they're smitten with me, and I just like them, then I'm upfront and honest with them about my intentions. I, too, have been on the other side, and only if God says to stay in this situation do I keep them in my life. We must heal properly and not build a relationship with someone who isn't equally caring for us.

Mark Twain once said, "Never allow someone to be your priority while allowing yourself to be their option," Once you can tell others about your failures or hurts, then you will understand your true mission in life.

We're here for you. We are praying for you. We're also celebrating your new life that is just around the corner. The next generation is depending on us surviving!

## PEACE OF GOD: 2021

Now, I can share additional the good news. In late April and early May of 2021, I was on a dating site, and I had given up. I had paid for three months, and it had been crazy. I had met some bozos. I didn't know some people thought it was a booty call website, and others were looking for a companion during the pandemic. People were lonely for a relationship. But I must testify, God had a plan. I responded to a gentleman that I had not answered and to let him know that I wasn't on the website anymore. See, the sites will keep your information to lure people into *liking* you even if you no longer pay for the site and have limited access. Okay, I'm not going to preach, but I have to say this. We wanted a true and unlimited relationship with Christ and our companion. Don't accept crumbs from others.

So, I was about to sign off, and I noticed some proud words about God on a gentleman's profile that came up after I responded to the other young man. This man was speaking about how great God was, and he wrote words of strength. I only texted amen. Then I received a match email from the website, which stated that we had a lot in common. When he saw the response on the website, the gentleman reached out to me.

He will tell you that he had met some crazy woman who said he loved God. Also, I had to be educated about a spiritual man and Christian. A spiritual man for the secular man was to pull a good woman, but he didn't have a relationship with God. Now, this is what I found out about the men I met on the website during COVID-19. It was no time to play around because COVID-19 was killing people and still claims lives today.

So, he texted me his phone number, which he never did, and I knew I wasn't giving out my number because of my past experiences. We talked for a while. We both had been ill with cancer and COVID-19 in the last year.

He also was alone in the state. God knew! We finally met, and most of our conversation was about God. We both had asked God for a companion who loved God and to share in our ministry. God, we didn't want to do it alone. We both loved to travel, but he wasn't a foodie, and I love going to expensive restaurants. Now, he thought I would be mad if funds got tight, but he didn't know I was a chef who could really cook so I won him over. Also, God was truly blessing me financially, so going out for dinner wouldn't be a problem! So, you buying this book just allowed me to go out to brunch this coming week.

What are your dreams?

Are you trust God?

Do you have hope from the story that I have shared with you?

# Thank You

I must thank God first for allowing me to live one more day. I thank you for allowing me to live and breathe every second. I thank God for growing back my hair. I thank God for my weight gain because I have the desire to eat, but I'm going to lose fifteen pounds because I'm getting married in December 2021! Yes! God did it. Let me say that we fell in love with God, and we fell in love with each other's spiritual size. Please let me make you laugh. Now, remember God had given me a beautiful home and the money to make the payments. God gave me a spiritual man but, remember a man too!

Now, where we both lived, we had such bad weather, and I had put my home up for sale. Then I got COVID-19 and had to hold off on selling the house while I was sick.

While I was sick, God brought a buyer who didn't even have a realtor. Now, I was still out sick with COVID-19, and I needed to get some sun, so I had walked to the front door to get that morning sun and talk to God. While God and I were talking, He spoke to me about the contract on my home. He told me to accept the bid for less than the listed price, as I would save $9,000 for the realtor commission because the person buying my home doesn't have a realtor. God planted the idea to sell my home and gave me direction on which buyer to choose. I sold my home. I kept seeking God and decided to retire from the corporate world to become a full-time minister and continue organizing retreats for those who help others but are empty inside. When you are hurting in silence, it comes out through your health. We are filling up hospitals with hurting people, and they're not getting well because of their lack of hope and strength.

Recall the cups and water illustration from the chapter "Sowing and Reaping." God tells us in His word that our blessing comes from an overflowing of joy, and if we are half empty or have no water, we are not trusting God and dying from within. I want you to start to allow your mind to *rest* for just five minutes. Then I would like you to *renew* your mind by thinking about the last time you were *joy* filled your cup. Now, write down what gave you this *joy* and what that feeling changed in you. We must continue to fill ourselves with joy. Speak out loud about the things you want to change and pray intentionally about those things. I told a few friends at the beginning of 2021 that I would get married this year. I said that I was going to give my all to the ministry and help others.

By the time this book is published, I will be a married woman. I'm marrying a minister who is on fire for God. We just established a nondenominational church, Beth El Worship Church. God has shown us both that if we trust Him and put Him first, He will, and has, given us the desires of our heart.

Peace of God

# HARVEST

What are your plans? List three goals you want to obtain.

A. _____

_____

_____

_____

_____

C. _____

_____

_____

_____

_____

D. _____

_____

_____

_____

_____

# WHAT IS YOUR ACTION PLAN?

30 days _____

_____

_____

_____

_____

_____

60 days _____

_____

_____

_____

_____

90 days _____

_____

_____

_____

_____

Journal each day of you mapping your
destiny to the new you.

# New Horizon

You may find gatherings of other individuals that have made a change in their lives by attending the *Rest Renew Restore* retreats on Facebook. Once you attend the retreats, you will attend *Belief Therapy* classes weekly to keep you mapping your *renewed* mind and *restore* all of your dreams.

CPSIA information can be obtained
at www.ICGtesting.com
Printed in the USA
BVHW040948290322
632742BV00010B/172